Mystery Mob
and the
UFO

Roger Hurn

Illustrated by
Stik

RISING ★ STARS

Rising Stars UK Ltd.
22 Grafton Street, London W1S 4EX
www.risingstars-uk.com

Published 2007
Reprinted 2008

Cover design: Button plc
Illustrator: Stik, Bill Greenhead for Illustration
Text design and typesetting: Andy Wilson
Publisher: Gill Budgell
Publishing manager: Sasha Morton
Editor: Catherine Baker
Series consultant: Cliff Moon

British Library Cataloguing in Publication Data.
A CIP record for this book is available from the British Library

ISBN: 978-1-84680-225-6

Printed in the UK by CPI Bookmarque, Croydon, CR0 4TD

Contents

Meet the Mystery Mob

Name:

Gummy

FYI: Gummy hasn't got much brain — and even fewer teeth.

Loves: Soup.

Hates: Toffee chews.

Fact: The brightest thing about him is his shirt.

Name:

Lee

FYI: If Lee was any cooler he'd be a cucumber.

Loves: Hip-hop.

Hates: Hopscotch.

Fact: He has his own designer label (which he peeled off a tin).

Name:

Rob

FYI: Rob lives in his own world – he's just visiting planet Earth.

Loves: Daydreaming.

Hates: Nightmares.

Fact: Rob always does his homework – he just forgets to write it down.

Name:

Dwayne

FYI: Dwayne is smarter than a tree full of owls.

Loves: Anything complicated.

Hates: Join-the-dots books.

Fact: If he was any brighter you could use him as a floodlight at football matches.

Name:

Chet

FYI: Chet is as brave as a lion with steel jaws.

Loves: Having adventures.

Hates: Knitting.

Fact: He's as tough as the chicken his granny cooks for his tea.

Name:

Adi

FYI: Adi is as happy as a football fan with tickets to the big match.

Loves: Telling jokes.

Hates: Moaning minnies.

Fact: He knows more jokes than a jumbo joke book.

Lights in the Sky

Something weird is going on.
Strange lights have been seen in the sky
above Witches Wood, near where
the Mystery Mob live.

Rob　　I reckon the lights must be from
　　　　a UFO.

Gummy　What's a UFO?

Dwayne　An Unidentified Flying Object.
　　　　It's a sort of alien spacecraft.

Chet   Yeah, maybe space aliens
          are about to land
          in their flying saucer.

Adi   Well, if they do,
          they'll have to leave it
          at a parking meteor.

Lee   Doh! Sometimes I wonder
          if you're from the same planet
          as the rest of us, Adi.

Rob   Too right. I think
he's from the moon.

Gummy Why?

Rob   Because he's a bit of a luna-tic!

Adi   Very funny. But at least
I'm not an astro-nut!

Chet   Hey, listen – I think we should go
to Witches Wood and check out
this UFO.

Dwayne   No can do. I've got to do
my homework.

Lee   And I've got football training.

Gummy   And I've got to go to the dentist.

Rob   And I'm grounded for putting
salt in my Dad's tea this morning
instead of sugar.

Adi   Well, I'm up for it.

Chet   You're on, mate!

Lee   And you can tell us
            all about it later tonight.

Chet and Adi

            Will do.

Chet and Adi head off to Witches Wood.

Little Green Man

Chet I bet I know where the UFO
has landed in Witches Wood.

Adi Where?

Chet Devil's Dell!

Adi But nobody ever goes there.
It's way too spooky.

Chet That's why it's the perfect spot
for a UFO to land.

The two boys creep along a narrow path.
They tiptoe past the trees
and crawl under bushes.
At last they come to Devil's Dell.
A large flying saucer is parked
on the grass.

Chet   I knew it. Look, there's the UFO.

Adi   Oh yeah! But where are
the aliens?

The boys hear a twig snap behind them.

Adi   Did you hear that?

Chet   I did. Do you think it's the aliens
creeping up on us?

Adi   Dunno. It could be anyone.
It could even be my mum!
Maybe she's come to fetch me
home for my tea.

Chet turns and looks.

Chet   I don't think so. Unless
your mum is three feet tall,
bald with a green head
and pointing a ray gun at us.

Adi   No, that's not her –
that sounds more like an alien.

Chet   Then we're in big trouble!

3

Kidnapped

The alien points at the UFO.
Then he waves his ray gun at the boys.

Adi   I think he wants us to go
on to the UFO.

Chet   He's going to kidnap us.

Adi   Maybe we'll end up in a zoo
on some strange alien planet!

Chet   Whatever. We'll think up a way
to escape.

Adi   That's easier said than done.
My brain went into hiding
when it saw that ray gun.

Chet   It's a pity *we* can't go
into hiding too.

Adi   Hey, what do you call an alien
with a ray gun?

Chet   I don't know.

Adi   Anything you like.
He can't speak English.

Chet   Doh … this is no time
for your daft jokes, Adi.

Alien   So you think I can't speak
English, then?

Adi   Er ... can you?

Chet   Well of course he can, Adi!
Just listen to him!

Adi   But ... how?

Alien   Well, my spaceship gets Sky TV.
Anyway – I will ask the questions!
You will be silent.

Adi   Er ... but if we're silent,
how do you expect us
to answer your questions?

Alien   Grrrr! Get on board or I'll shoot.

Adi   All right. Keep your hair on.
        Oops, sorry. You haven't got any.

The alien waves his ray gun at the boys.
They look at each other, then climb
on board the spaceship.

Alien   You are my prisoners now!

Things are looking very grim for Chet
and Adi.

Space Invaders

The inside of the UFO is very hi-tech.
There are computer screens everywhere.

Chet   Wow. This UFO is just so cool.

Adi   Yeah, but I reckon
we're in hot water.

Chet   Too right. We need to
find out the alien's plan for us.

Adi   Hey, Mr Spaceman.
        What are you up to?
        Why have you come to Earth?

Alien   I was sent from Planet Zargon
          to spy on you humans.
          But now my mission is over.

Chet   Why's that?

Alien   You humans are weak.
          You're no match for us.
          So I'm going to send a signal
          to my planet's space fleet.

Adi   Er … what kind of signal?

Alien   A signal to invade Earth,
            of course! We will show no mercy!

The alien laughs. He thinks he's won.
But Chet and Adi are not beaten yet.
Adi has a plan.

Chet   Don't send the signal,
             Mr Spaceman. If you do,
             you'll be making a big mistake.

Adi   That's right. We humans
             are weak, but the gastropods
             aren't.

Alien   Gastropods? What are they?

Chet looks at Adi. He has no idea either.

Adi   (winking at Chet) They're huge monsters that live under the sea. They come out at night to hunt us. Then they suck out our brains. There's nothing we can do to stop them.

Chet   But maybe you aliens can beat them.

Alien   Of course we can! We'll zap them with our ray guns!

Adi   That won't work. A gastropod
            has a really thick skin.

Chet   That's right. Your ray guns
            will only tickle it.

Adi   And you can't tickle a gastropod
            to death.

The alien takes out a round metal ball
from a cupboard.

Alien   Ha! Those gastropods
            won't be laughing
            when they see this!

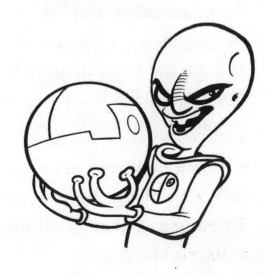

Chet   What is it?

Alien   It's a mega bomb.
We'll use it to blow up
the gastropods.

Adi   That bomb's no good.
The gastropods will play
football with it.

Chet   Yes. They love football
but they never get to play –
their claws keep bursting the ball.
But your metal mega bomb
is just right.

Adi   They'll have a match –
gastropods versus aliens.

Chet   They'll put you in goal
for the penalty shoot out.

Adi   But when you save the ball –
it'll explode!

Chet   And they'll be singing,
"One-nil to the gastropods".

Adi   And you'll be blown
over the crossbar
and all the way back up
into space.

Chet   Only without your UFO.

Adi   Nasty.

Chet   Very nasty.

The space alien looks very worried.
The boys cross their fingers.
Will their plan work?

5

Game Over

The space alien tells the boys
not to move. He presses a button
and a computer lights up.
The chief alien appears on the screen.

Chief alien

> Well, Zarg – what did you
> find out on Earth?
> Should our fleet invade?

Alien   No, sir! The Earth is too
dangerous! The humans
are weak, but you should see
the gastropods! They'd eat us
for breakfast!

The alien tells the chief alien
about the gastropods. The chief alien
turns bright green.

Chief alien

Zarg, you must return at once!

Alien   Yes, sir.

Chief alien

We will find a safer planet
to invade.

Meanwhile, Chet and Adi are whispering.

Chet   Come on, Adi.
Let's get out of here
while his back's turned.

Adi   I'm already gone!

The boys jump out of the UFO
and race off into the bushes.
The alien doesn't try to catch them.
It's getting dark and he's scared
he might bump into a gastropod.
He starts up the engine. The UFO
spins round and round then shoots off
up into space.

Adi   Let's hope we've seen
the last of him.

Chet   He won't be back.
He swallowed our story.

Adi   Well, it's better than being
swallowed by a gastropod.

Chet   Adi, gastropods don't really exist,
do they? Tell me it was just a fib
you made up to fool the alien.

Adi	Sure. I'm good at fibbing.
Chet	And they don't come out of the sea to hunt humans at night?
Adi	No way.
Chet	Thank goodness for that.
Adi	Why?

Chet   Because I thought I saw one
sneaking about over there.

Adi   Chet …

Chet   What's up?

Adi   I know you're winding me up,
but …

Chet   But what?

Adi   It's late. It's dark.
         And I want my tea,
         so let's ruuuuuun!

The two boys race off home.
In Devil's Dell nothing moves –
not even a gastropod.

About the author

Roger Hurn has:

- been an actor in 'The Exploding Trouser Company'
- played bass guitar in a rock band
- been given the title Malam Oga (wise teacher, big boss!) while on a storytelling trip to Africa.

Now he's a writer, and he hopes you like reading about the Mystery Mob as much as he likes writing about them.

Outer space quiz

Questions

1 What can you find at the centre of gravity?

2 What do you get if you cross a comet with a cod?

3 How many balls of string do you need to reach the moon?

4 Why didn't the astronaut get burnt when he landed on the Sun?

5 Which chocolate bars do astronauts like best?

6 How does the solar system hold up its trousers?

7 How do you know when Saturn's had a bath?

8 What's the opposite of a meteorite?

How did you score?

✋ If you got all eight outer space answers
   correct, then you are ready for infinity
   and beyond!

✋ If you got six outer space answers correct,
   then you're almost ready for blast off.

✋ If you got fewer than four outer space
   answers correct, then you're a space cadet,
   not an astronaut.

When I was a kid

Question When you were a kid,
did you want to be an astronaut
when you grew up?

Roger Not really.

Question Why not?

Roger Because I'm scared of heights –
and that's bad news if you want
to be an astronaut.

Question Have you ever seen a UFO?

Roger No, but I'm a rotten cook
so I've seen lots of unidentified
frying objects in my kitchen!

Question If you could go up into space,
where would you go?

Roger Well, I wouldn't go to the moon.
I don't think it would be much fun.

Question Why not?

Roger It hasn't got any atmosphere.

Adi's favourite UFO joke

What do you call a wizard in a UFO?

A Flying Sorcerer!

What not to do if you meet an alien

 Don't try to shake hands with an alien – it may have tentacles.

 Don't offer an alien a Mars Bar. It won't make it feel at home.

 Don't say, "What on Earth are you doing here?"

 Don't tell a hungry alien that it can't eat until launch time.

 Don't say: "You must be over the moon to have landed on Earth."

 Don't tell a thirsty alien it can get a drink at the space bar on your computer.

Don't offer it your mobile phone
so it can call home – it'll cost you a fortune!

 Don't ask an alien from the planet Saturn
to give you a ring sometime.

 Don't ask an alien robot if it shaves
with a laser blade.

Fantastic facts about space

1   There are eight main planets in our solar system: Mercury, Venus, Earth, Mars, Jupiter, Saturn, Uranus and Neptune – but not Pluto.

2   Scientists say Pluto is only a dwarf planet, but some people think it's Mickey Mouse's dog.

3   Our Sun is a star – even though it's never had its own TV show.

4   The Sun is over one million times bigger than the Earth. It just looks small to us because it's so far away.

5   Astronauts on the International Space Station recycle the contents from the onboard toilet into water pure enough to drink – yuk!

Space lingo

Anti-gravity A place free from the force of gravity – not one of your female relatives.

Flying saucer An alien spaceship – not what a football manager throws when he's lost his temper.

Man in the Moon When the moon is full it looks like a man's face. When the first rocket landed there it was one in the eye for the man in the moon.

Outer space Everything beyond the Earth's atmosphere. There's almost as much space in outer space as there is inside Gummy's head.

Rings of Saturn These are rings of water ice that circle the planet Saturn. They are not bling-bling!

Rocket A spacecraft – not a big telling off from your teacher.

Mystery Mob

Mystery Mob Set 1:

Mystery Mob and the Abominable Snowman
Mystery Mob and the Big Match
Mystery Mob and the Circus of Doom
Mystery Mob and the Creepy Castle
Mystery Mob and the Haunted Attic
Mystery Mob and the Hidden Treasure
Mystery Mob and the Magic Bottle
Mystery Mob and the Missing Millions
Mystery Mob and the Monster on the Moor
Mystery Mob and the Mummy's Curse
Mystery Mob and the Time Machine
Mystery Mob and the UFO

Mystery Mob Set 2:

Mystery Mob and the Ghost Town
Mystery Mob and the Bonfire Night Plot
Mystery Mob and the April Fools' Day Joker
Mystery Mob and the Great Pancake Race
Mystery Mob and the Scary Santa
Mystery Mob and the Conker Conspiracy
Mystery Mob and the Top Talent Contest
Mystery Mob and Midnight at the Waxworks
Mystery Mob and the Runaway Train
Mystery Mob and the Wrong Robot
Mystery Mob and the Day of the Dinosaurs
Mystery Mob and the Man Eating Tiger

RISING★STARS